# A SPOKEN WORD

---

## TYWANA R. FREDENBURG

PUBLISHED BY FASTPENCIL

Published by FastPencil
307 Orchard City Drive
Suite 210
Campbell CA 95008 USA
info@fastpencil.com
(408) 540-7571
(408) 540-7572 (Fax)
http://www.fastpencil.com

Printed in the United States of America.

First Edition

I would like to dedicate this book to my loving children and husband. Thank you so much for your love and your support. I pray and hope that this book would encourage you to speak the Word of God. We all may reach a point of which we call disappointment in our lives and even may feel like throwing in the towel. Just remember that God knows all and he will never leave you nor forsake you. I pray that you will never give up on God and that you will always believe in His Spoken Word. Mommy loves you and daddy very much.

ॐ

# Acknowledgments

I would like to thank my husband for his support while completing the book. I would like to thank my mother, Earline McClure Wyatt who has always taught me to speak the word of God and to trust him no matter how things look. I thank God for all of my siblings, TiNing, Leonard, and Laqeita for their love, support, and encouragement. I would like to thank my god parents, Edward and Catherine Thomas for their love, support, and prayers. I thank God for my Grandma Peaches for showing me the love of God, for her prayers, and for sharing her testimonies. I thank God for my god sister for her prayers. I would like to thank my pastors, Bishop King and the late first lady Mother King, Pastor Rod Parsley and his lovely wife Joni for their teachings. I thank my editor Marcus Cylar for editing the book. Thank you Elder Kellen Brooks for referring editor Marcus Cylar. Thank you Julie Falk for the lovely cover photo. I thank God for these wonderful testimonies that he's blessed me with and for giving me a "A Spoken Word"!

# CONTENTS

# 1

## DO YOU REMEMBER?

Stop and take a minute to think about every word the Lord has spoken to you. Think about all the wonderful promises he's made to you throughout your life! So many of you have had prophecies spoken over your life and continue to wait for them to be fulfilled.

Today, I would like to speak a powerful word to you, to BELIEVE and DON'T GIVE UP! Numbers 23:19 reads, "God is not a man, that he should lie; neither the son of man, that he should repent: hath he said, and shall he not do it? or hath he spoken, and shall he not make it good?" This scripture confirms and secures all of his promises and every word he's ever spoken or will ever speak.

Allow me to share with you about a strategic time in my life where the Holy Spirit spoke a word that increased my faith dramatically. During the 2000-01 school year, I faced a time of destitution in my life like never before. I was in desperate need of an enormous *financial* blessing to be able to continue my college education. For a moment, it seemed as if my finances were all dried up. Deep within, I knew I had nothing to stand on but my faith and the word of God. During this time, I desperately sought the *Lord's* face for instruction for my life. *Overrides* were given to attend classes since my bills were not yet paid. I recall the dorm attendant shouting out my name every time I passed by the front desk in the lobby saying, "We'll be coming up to change the locks to your room soon." I remember what I felt every time I *heard* those words. I felt fear, embarrassment, and a feeling that God had abandoned me.

I had to shake myself, remembering the word of the Lord from Ephesians 3:20: "Now unto him who is able to do abundantly above all that we ask or think, according to the power that worketh in us," Matthew 6:26: "And behold the fouls of the air; for they sew not, neither do they reap, nor gather into barns; yet your heavenly father feedeth them. Are you not much better than they?" and Isaiah 26:3 "You will keep in perfect peace those whose minds are steadfast, because they trust in you." I remember sharing my situation with one of the counselors/mentors on campus, thinking that I would receive some encouragement. However, she stated, "Honey, just drop out this semester. Your God can only do so much." I stood in shock that she would allow those words to come out of her mouth about my God. I looked her dead in the eye, pointed my finger at her, and said, "My God will provide and you will see, and when he does this thing for me, I will be back to tell you personally what he's done and how he did it."

God spoke to me early one morning and told me to get up and anoint my room and my threshold. Out of obedience, I got up and did what the Lord instructed me to do. It is always important to follow the God's instructions. A few weekends later, I decided to go home and visit my family. When I returned back to my dorm, I found some of my fellow classmates standing outside their rooms, not able to enter in. One gentleman called out my name and said, "Tywana, you better check your lock, they came up and changed our locks." I remember sighing to myself saying, "Oh Jesus." I stuck my key in the hole and turned to the right. I *heard* a click and the door pushed opened. I began to praise God. It was that moment when God spoke to me and said, remember when I woke you early in the morning to anoint your dorm room and threshold?" I responded, "Yes," he then proceeded to tell me he gave me them instructions so the locksmith would pass my room by like death *passed* by the children of Israel, in Exodus 12:13: "The blood will be a sign for you on the houses where you are, and when I see the blood, I will pass over you. No destructive plague will touch you when I strike Egypt."

God did exactly what he said he would do, with not only one blessing, but two in one. He sent my father to pay my bill for not just one semester but three. God also restored our father-daughter relationship. How can I forget, while I was seeking God for instructions during this storm, he showed me my unsaved father at the time, wearing a ministerial collar, praying over me right before my breakthrough. God is good. God has a plan for each of us and he's called us all for something. It was amazing how God was with me every step of the way. I returned back to the counselor/mentor the same day God blessed me, like I said I would. I told her what the Lord had done for me. She sat there in her seat in shock. Then she stated, "well good for you." I shouted, "Our God is faithful." In our storms, we have to always remember to heed to the voice of the Lord and his instruction. So many people had wonderful *humanistic* ideas or instructions for me during this time. But God already had a plan for me to make it through the storm before I encountered it. There were a lot of people instructing me to go home and get another job to pay the balance of my bill. However, I knew if I sat out for a *semester,* I wouldn't have the *will-power* to return. The Lord spoke to me from Exodus 14:13, "And Moses said unto the people, fear ye not, stand still, and see the salvation of the LORD, which he would shew to you to day: for the Egyptians whom ye have seen to day, ye shall see them again no more for ever." God's plan is always to prosper us and to give us an expected end. I followed God's plan and I graduated December 2003.

# 2

---

## WHAT HAS GOD
## SPOKEN TO YOU?

In Exodus 3, God spoke to Moses out of a
burning bush. Exodus 3:7-10 "The Lord said,
"I have indeed seen the misery of my people
in Egypt. I have heard them crying because of
their slave drivers, and I am concerned about
their sufferings. So, I have come down to
rescue them from the hand of the Egyptians and to bring them up out of that land
into a good and spacious land, a land flowing
with milk and honey—the home of the Canaanites, Hitties, Amorites, Perizzites, Hivites
and Jebusites. And now the cry of the Israelites has reached me, and I have seen the way

the Egyptians are oppressing them. So now, go. I am sending you to pharaoh to bring my people the Israelites out of Egypt."

At the very moment God had spoken to Moses, the Children of Israel *were* already set free. The moment God spoke the word, it was done! God knew when Moses was born that he would raise him up to lead his people out of Egypt. There was a cry and God *heard* that cry. The more the Israelite became oppressed, the stronger they grew. God had a plan for his people at the beginning of time. Exodus 3:16-17 says, "Go, assemble the elders of Israel and say to them, The Lord, the God of your father's the God of Abraham, Isaac and the God of Jacob-has appeared to me and said: I have watched over you and has seen what has been done to you in Egypt. And I have promised to bring you up out of your misery in Egypt into the land of the Caanites, Hittites, Amorutes, Perzzites, Hivites, and Jebusites—a land flowing with milk and honey."

Jeremiah 29:11 tells us that God has plans to prosper us and not to harm us, plans to give you hope and a future and an expected end. God had a plan for the Israelites before they were even taken into captivity. This reminds me of how God had a plan to redeem us while we were yet in our sins. When Adam and Eve *disobeyed* God's command to not eat from the tree of the knowledge of good and evil, they were kicked out of the Garden of Eden for their disobedience. This was considered to be the fall of man. God had to then establish a plan to redeem his people. So, God sent his son Jesus to be a sacrifice for our sins. However, when Jesus came down to be the *ultimate* sacrifice, we were yet sinners. He came to make a way of escape for us. God is always making a way of escape for his people. If you journey through the word of God, you will discover how he made a way of escape for many of his people.

Moses' life was changed the very moment he heard a word from God in the burning bush. His mindset, life, and position *were* changed. He was no longer Moses being trained to lead the *Israelites*, he was Moses, the leader of the *Israelites*. Just as God changed Moses' position, he is getting ready to change your position. God is getting ready to increase your faith, change your circumstances, and change your life forever! From this day forward, I declare, in the name of Jesus, that your life will never be the same. Even your thought patterns will be different. God is ready to renew your mind through his word. Just one spoken word from God will change your life forever.

Just as God was with Moses, God is with you today! What is it that God is telling you right now? What has God said he's getting ready to do for you? God called Moses and qualified him to go free the children of Israel. Moses was being trained since birth to lead the *Israelites*. He was notified of his job description at the Horeb Mountain from the *fiery* bush. Let me tell you, your *miracle*, that blessing you need that you cry out for, has already been ordained for you by God. Your position in Christ has already been established, for God knows your beginning and your end. The Lord saw the misery of his people and qualified Moses to lead them out from their misery. Put your trust in the Lord; the very thing *you're* facing today is for God to get the Glory. He's in control of all things.

Proverbs 3:5-6 tells us to "Trust in the Lord with all our heart and lean not on our own understanding; In all your ways acknowledge him and he will make your paths straight. When you trust in the Lord he will direct your paths." Moses was a man who had a very bad *stuttering* problem. Moses didn't believe God could use him to speak to the children of Israel with his speech impediment. Moses asked for Aaron to go with him to speak and God still used him. Moses' speech impediment didn't change God's mind for the mission he had for Moses. God still had a plan to use Moses to deliver his people out of *Egypt*. Many of you today have allowed fear to take a hold of you. I would like to come into agreement with you right now and bind the spirit of fear in your life. My Bible tells me in *Matthew* 18:18, "*Truly* I tell you; whatever you bind on earth will be bound in heaven, and whatever you loose on earth will be loosed in heaven." God had an assignment for Moses, just as he has an assignment for you. We must always remember God is strong in our weaknesses. Moses' weakness was his speech. God showed himself strong through Moses speech impediment. Allow him to do the same in you.

# 3

## IT IS WELL WITH MY SOUL!

2 Kings 4:8-17 talks *about* a *Shunam-mitewoman* that saw a need for the man of God, Elisha. "One day Elisha went to Shunem. And a well-to-do woman was there, who urged him to stay for a meal. So whenever he came by, he stopped there to eat. She said to her husband, 'I know that this man who often comes our way is a holy man of God. Let's make a small room on the roof and put in it a bed and a table, a chair and a lamp for him. Then he can stay there whenever he comes to us. One day when Elisha came, he went up to his room and lay down there. He

said to his servant Gehazi, 'Call the Shunammite.' So he called her, and she stood before
him. Elisha said to him, 'Tell her, 'You have
gone to all this trouble for us. Now what can
be done for you? Can we speak on your
behalf to the King or the commander of the
army?' She replied, "I have a home among my
own people.' What can be done for her?'
Elisha asked. Gehazi said, 'Well, she has no
son and her husband is old.' Then Elisha said,
'Call her.' So he called her, and she stood in
the doorway. 'About this time next year, '
Elisha said, 'you will hold a son in your arms.'
'No, my lord,' she objected. 'Don't mislead
your servant, O man of God!' But the woman
became pregnant, and the next year about
that same time she gave birth to a son, just as
Elisha had told her."

In this story, you see that Elisha was a prophet
who often came through the town to conduct
*revivals*. This Shunammite *woman* invited Elisha
into her home for dinner when he was in town.
What this Shunammite *woman* was doing was

making a deposit into Elisha's life. Do you know when you make a *deposit*, you can make a withdrawal? The Shunammite women had shown compassion and a desire to care for the man of God. By caring for him, she was making a deposit into his life. Little did the Shunammite *woman* know that as she was making a *deposit,* the Lord had ordained a withdrawal for her. This Shunammite *woman* was being set up for a blessing from God. Elisha had a need, and the *Shunammite woman* saw the need and began to fulfill the need for the man of God. The *woman* had a conversation with her husband regarding preparing a room for the man of God. She said, "Let's put a room on the roof with a bed, table, chair and a lamp for him." In this room, Elisha was able to rest and regain his strength back after ministering to God's people.

**Elisha carried an *anointing. Anointing* means "smearing". Elisha was an *anointed* prophet of God. Whatever he touched he smeared the *anointing* upon. The *anointing* was smeared upon Elisha's room, bed, and clothes. Whenever Elisha left out of his room, the *anointing* remained. Elisha paid attention to all the preparation the Shunammite *woman* had made for him. When he asked her what she needed, the *woman* replied, "I live *amongst* my own people." She didn't want to disclose her need to Elisha. However, Elisha turned and asked his servant Gehazi what it was the *woman* needed. Gehazi *answered* and said her husband is *too* old and she wants a baby. Elisha turned and looked at the *woman* and spoke: "by this time next year you will be holding a baby." The *woman* replied, "don't play with me." It was clear by her response the *woman* had faced some disappointments in her life concerning a child. However, when God speaks a word, we know that it shall come to pass. As soon as Elisha spoke the word to the Shunammite *woman*, it was done. The word of God went out to accomplish what needed. There is power in what you speak. Around the time Elisha said that she would be holding a child is when her *miracle* was birthed.

2Kings 4:18-36 *explains* how the Shunammite *woman's* promise died. "The child grew, and one day he went out to his father, who was with the reapers. "My head!" he said to his father. His father told a servant, "Carry him to his mother." After the servant had lifted him up and carried him to his mother, the boy sat on her lap until noon, and then he died. She went up and laid him on the bed of the man of God, then shut the door and went out. She called her husband and said. "Please send me one of the servants and a donkey so I can go to the man of God quickly and return." "Why go to him today?" he asked. "It's not the New Moon or the Sabbath." "It's all right," she said. She saddled the donkey and said to her servant, "Lend on; don't slow down for me unless I tell you." So she set out and came to the man of God at Mount Carmel. When he saw her in the distance, the man of God said to his servant Gehazi, "Look! There's the Shunammite! Run to meet her and ask her, 'Are you all right? Is your child alright?'" "Everything is all right," she said. When she reached the man of God at the mountain, she took hold of his feet. Gehazi came over to push her away, but the man of God said, "Leave her alone! She is in bitter distress, but the Lord has hidden it from me and has not told me why." "Did I ask you for a son, my lord?" she

said. "Didn't I tell you, 'Don't raise my hopes'?"
Elisha said to Gehazi, "Tuck your cloak into your
belt, take my staff in your hand and run. If you
meet anyone, do not greet him, and if anyone
greets you, do not answer. Lay my staff on the
boy's face. " But the child's mother said," As
surely as the Lord lives and as you live, I will not
leave you." So he got up and followed her. Gehazi
went on ahead and laid the staff on the boy's face,
but there was no sound or response. So Gehazi
went back to meet *Elisha* and told him, "The boy
has not awakened." When Elisha reached the
house, there was the boy lying dead on his
couch. He went in, shut the door on the two of
them and prayed to the Lord. Then he got on the
bed and lay upon the boy, mouth to mouth, eyes
to eyes, hands to hands. As he stretched himself
out upon him, the boy's body grew warm. Elisha
turned away and walked back and forth in the
room and then got on the bed and stretched out
upon him once more. The boy sneezed seven
times and opened his eyes. Elisha summoned
Gehazi and said, " Call the Shunammite." And he
did. When she came, he said, "Take your
son." She came in, fell at his feet and bowed to

the ground. Then she took her son and went out."

In the same chapter, it reads that the Shunammite *woman's* promise had died after she received it. However, God is still a promise keeper. The Shunammite woman's son, her promise, had grown older. One day, he was working in the field with his father, he had a headache. He ran and told his father and the reapers. His father asked the reapers to take him to his mother. The boy sat on her lap and then died. Some of you have had dreams, promises given, and prayers answered, only to watch your blessing die or crumble right before your eyes. When the *Shunammitewoman's* son died, she took him up to Elisha's room, the room where the *anointing* was smeared. She laid him in the *anointing*, Elisha's bed. Then she left out of the room and shut the door. She shut her promise in the *anointing*. The mother then told her husband to saddle up her donkey. The *woman* was running to get Elisha. The Shunammite *woman* refused to let her promise die. She refused to believe her promise was gone. The Shunammite *woman's* promise lived. Speak life to your situation, dreams, and promises by speaking the word of God.

# 4

## God is a Promise Keeper!

### God's Covenant with Noah

In Genesis, God made a covenant with Abraham.

The definition of agreement is:

1. an agreement, usu. formal, between two or more persons to do or not do something specified.

2. The conditional promises made to humanity by God, as revealed in Scripture.

3. a formal agreement of legal validity, esp. one under seal.

4. To enter into a covenant

5. to promise by covenant; pledge.

6. to stipulate.

Genesis 12:1-3 The Lord had said to Abram, "Go from your country, your people and your father's household to the land I will show you." I will make you into a great nation and I will bless you; I will make your name great, and you will be a blessing . I will bless those who bless you, and whoever curses you I will curse,' and all peoples on earth will be blessed through you.

God made a promise to Abraham in verses 1-3. God's word is true. God continues to make his covenant with Abraham *throughout* the book of Genesis.

Genesis 17:1-27 When Abram was ninety-nine years old, the Lord appeared to him and said, "I am God Almighty, walk before me faithfully and be blameless. Then I will make my covenant between me and you and will greatly increase you numbers." Abram fell face down, and God said to him, "As for me, this is my covenant with you: You will be the father of many nations. No longer will you be called Abram; your name will be Abraham, for I have made you a father of many nations. I will make you very fruitful; I will make nations of you, and kings will come from you. I will establish my covenant as an everlasting covenant between me and you and your descendants after you for the generations to come, to be your God and the God of your descendants after you for the generations to come, to be your God and the God of your descendants after you. the Whole land of Canaan, where you now reside as a foreigner, I will give as an everlasting possession to you and your descendants after you; and I will be their God." Then God said to Abraham, "As for you, you must keep my covenant, you and your descendants after you for the generations to come. This is my covenant with you and your descendants after you, the covenant you are to keep: Every male among you shall be circumcised, including those born in your household or bought with money from a foreigner—those who are not your offspring. Whether born in your *household* or bought with your money, they must be circumcised. My covenant in your flesh is to be an everlasting covenant. Any uncircumcised male, who has not been circumcised in the flesh, will be cut off from his people; he has broken my covenant." God also said to Abraham, "As for Sarai your wife, you are no longer to call her

Sarai; her name will be Sarah. I will bless her and will surely give you a son by her. I will bless her so that she will be the mother of nations, Kings of peoples will come from her." Abraham fell face-down; he laughed and said to himself, "Will a son be born to a man a hundred years old? Will Sarah bear a child at the age of ninety?" And Abraham sad to God, "If only Ishmael might live under your blessing!" Then God said, "Yes, but your wife Sarah will bear you a son, and you will call him Isaac. I will establish my covenant with him as an everlasting covenant for his descendants after him. And as for Ishmael, I have heard you: I will surely bless him; I will make him fruitful and will greatly increase his numbers. He will be the father of twelve rulers, and I will make him into a great nation. But my covenant I will establish with Isaac, whom Sarah will bear to you by this time next year. When he had finished speaking with Abraham, God went up from him. On that very day Abraham took his son Ishmael and all those born in his household or bought with his money, every male in his household, and circum-cised them as God told him. Abraham was ninety-nine years old when he was circumcised, and his son Ishmael was thirteen; Abraham and his son Ishmael were both circumcised on that very day. And every male in Abraham's household, including those born in his household or bought from a foreigner, was circumcised with him.

**God did for Sarah what he said he would do!**

Genesis 21:1-6 Now the Lord was gracious to Sarah as he had said, and the Lord did for Sarah what he had promised. Sarah became pregnant and bore a son to Abraham in his old age, at the very time God had promised him. Abraham was a hundred years old, Abraham circumcised him, as God commanded him. Abraham was a hundred years old when his son Issac was born to him. Sarah said, "God has brought me laughter, and everyone who hears about this will laugh with me. "And she added, "Who would have said to Abraham that Sarah would nurse children? Yet I have borne him a son in his old age.

The bible tells us in Numbers 23; 19 God is not human, that he should lie, not a human being, that he should change his mind. Does he speak and then not act? Does he promise and not fulfill?

Titus 1:2 In the hope of eternal life which God, who does not lie, promised before the beginning of time. God is not a man that he should lie or change his mind. This is a good time to shout right here! God is a promise keeper. Whatever he has SPOKEN to you through dreams, words, or through prophesies, it shall come to pass.

In Genesis 9:9, God made his covenant with Noah. "I now establish my covenant with you and with your descendants after you and with every living creature that was with you—birds, the livestock and all the wild animals, all those that came out of the ark with you-every living creature on earth. I establish my covenant with you: Never again will all life be destroyed by the water of the a flood; never again will there be a flood to destroy the earth. A sign of the covenant was established between God and all life on the earth—the rainbow. God said every time he brings the clouds over the earth and the rainbow appears in the clouds will be a reminder of the covenant.

**The Israelites**

Exodus 3:17 "And I have promised to bring you up out of your misery in Egypt into the land of the Canaanites, Hittites, Amorites, Perizzites, Hivites and Jebusites-a land flowing with milk and honey." Those of you that are going through a storm in your life, get ready get ready get ready! God is getting ready to bring you out. You are getting ready to see the sun shine again. You are getting ready to experience the promises of the Lord that he's had for you since the beginning of time.

One morning in prayer God spoke to me and said There is a release a release of his spirit, healing, finances, and salvation. There is a release! God is taking you to a place were you never been before. He's paving the way for you. He's placing his Glory upon you. The people will see the glory of the Lord. God said he's taking his people from the pit to the palace to the house of Royalty, just like he did Joseph in Genesis 41;41. God said he's breaking up the harden hearts and he's softening the hearts. God said the grounds is breaking up and their is a release. He's removing our infirmities. God said trust him. He will lead and guide your feet. He said trust him.

He has placed favour upon your life. He said he's destroying the adversaries in your life. He's destroying the bands of wickedness. He's healing the broken hearted. There is a release of God's Spirit. He's pouring his spirit out upon you. God says his plan is to prosper you. When the enemy tried to destroy you and you thought you were all alone, God was there protecting you. He had and still has a plan to prosper you. God Says where he leads you because of the anointing people will be set free. What God is getting ready to do in your life is going to blow your natural born mind. There is a release the grounds are breaking. Get ready! God made a promise to bring his people up out of their miseries. You can't stay in the same place forever!

Numbers 10:29 Now Moses said to Hobab son Reuel the Midianite, Moses father-in-law, We are setting out for the place about which the Lord said , 'I will give it to you.' Come with us and we will treat you well, for the Lord has promised good things to Israel."

Joshua 21:45 Not one of all the LORD's good promises to Israel failed; every one was fulfilled. God is a promise Keeper!

Deuteronomy 15:6 For the Lord your God will bless you as he has promised, and you will lend to many nations but will borrow from none. You will rule over many nations but none will rule over you.

# 5

## SPEAK TO THAT MOUNTAIN!

It is important to speak life. God has given us the power and authority to speak to the mountains that stand in our way. However, in order to speak to the mountains, we must have faith that the mountain will move. Hebrews 11:1 reads, "Now faith is the confidence in what we hope for and the assurance about what we do not see." Two words describe faith: confidence and assurance. These two qualities need a secure beginning and ending point. The beginning point of faith is believing in God's character—*he is who he says he is.*** The end point is believing in God's promises—*he will do what he says he will do.* When we believe that God will fulfill his promises, even though we don't see those promises materializing yet, we demonstrate true faith. Hebrews 11:3 says, "By faith we understand that the universe was formed at God's command, so that what is seen was not made out of what was visible." It was by faith that God called the universe into existence out of nothing; he declared that it was to be, and it was. Our faith is in God who created the entire universe by his word. God's word has awesome power.

Matthew 17:14-20, When they came to the crowd, a man approached Jesus and knelt before him. "Lord, have mercy on my son ," he said. " He has seizures and is suffering greatly. He often falls into the fire or into the water. I brought him to your disciples, but they could not heal him." "You unbelieving and perverse generation," Jesus replied, "How long shall I stay with you? How long shall I put up with you? Bring the boy here to me." Jesus rebuked the demon, and it came out of the boy, and he was healed at that moment. JESUS SPOKE AND IT HAPPENED!

FAITH!*** Then the disciples came to Jesus in private and asked, "Why couldn't we drive it out? He replied, "Because you have little faith. Truly I tell you, if you have faith as small as a mustard seed you can say to this mountain, Move from here to there and it will move. Nothing will be impossible for you.

# Conclusion: Speaking the Word of God!

We are living in a time where many people are believing and speaking the things of this world. God wants us to speak *His Word*. Proverbs 18:21 states, "Death and life are in the power of the tongue: and they that love it shall eat the fruit thereof." We have the *ability* to speak life or death over our situations. When you rise in the morning, *command* your day. Declare your peace of mind, favor, blessings and protection. Declare God's word over your life. Romans 12:2 tells us to "Be not conformed to this world: but be ye transformed by the renewing of your mind, that ye may prove what is that good, and acceptable, and perfect, will of God."

I remember when my husband and I were trying to have children. The first time I was informed that I was pregnant the doctor stated that it was an unhealthy pregnancy. I was informed that I was having a miscarriage. I remember praying and believing God that the baby, our seed, would live. However, the struggle continued. I remember my mother coming over to the house to be with us during that difficult time in our lives. Although my blood count for the baby continued to decrease we continued to believe God and speak his word. While speaking God's word, the doctors were operating in the natural, speaking only what they seen, a miscarriage occurring. It became harder to believe God because I was surrounded by doubt. People approached me stating, "at least you didn't have a chance to see your child. Just try again." Hearing those words tore me to pieces. However, I believe people didn't really know what to say during that time of tragedy for my husband and I. The pain was great both spiritually and naturally. There was a time during the miscarriage I passed out due to the loss of blood and pain. My mother was trying to keep me responsive the best way she knew how. She began to pray over me and my husband placed a cold rag over my forehead. I was placed on bed rest until I was strong enough to get around. The saints came to visit me. I was so depressed and hurt at the time. My husband and I continued to try to have children. The doctors wanted to do a procedure on me to help me conceive. However, I remember on my way to the doctors' office praying quoting God back his word with tears in my eyes. I trust you Lord. God is able to do exceedingly above all we ask or even think according to the power that works on the inside of us. To make the long story short, the procedure was unsuccessful that day because the doctor stated I was PREGNANT! After four years of trying to conceive I was PREGNANT! God had blessed us to conceive. Not truly understanding why I had to go through something that difficult. What I have found out is what I went through was not for myself but for others. After having a miscarriage God placed other women in my life that has had miscarriages and I was able to pray for them remembering the pain I experienced both naturally and spiritually. I was able to pray a sincere prayer as if it was me again trying to conceive. I can testify that all of those women God told me to pray for have children today. The first women I prayed for conceived three months later after praying for her. God instructs us in his word to be fruitful and multiply. We all need our minds to be renewed and transformed like Christ to be able to speak and have faith in his spoken word.

Speak life over all your situations. God has a plan to prosper each and every *one* of us and to give us an expected end. We just have to trust him. I imagine that it had to be quite difficult for Noah to believe it was getting ready to rain since Noah had never seen rain. However, Noah *began* to warn the people about the word that God had shared with him. "It's going to rain." However, because of the people's unbelief, they perished. Although it may have sounded strange, Noah chose to believe God, and by doing so, he reaped the *benefits*. Noah's family and the animals God had Noah rescue survived. As believers, if we want to survive, we must believe and speak the word of God. No matter what we face in life, God always gives instructions on what to do. Today, we ask God for ears to hear and eyes to see so that we hear his voice clearly and see the plan that he has for us. Always remember, Numbers 23:19 tells us that, "God is not a man, that he should lie; neither the son of man, that he should repent: hath he said, and shall he not do it? or hath he spoken, and shall he not make it good?" We must speak God's word back to him. Remind God of his word. It is "Impossible for God to do Nothing!"***

CPSIA information can be obtained
at www.ICGtesting.com
Printed in the USA
LVOW03s2057220517
535476LV00010B/73/P